THE DAILY STRUGGLE OF THOSE WHO LIVED IN THE MIDDLE AGES

Ancient History Books for Kids | Children's Ancient History

Speedy Publishing LLC
40 E. Main St. #1156
Newark, DE 19711
www.speedypublishing.com
Copyright 2017

All Rights reserved. No part of this book may be reproduced or used in any way or form or by any means whether electronic or mechanical, this means that you cannot record or photocopy any material ideas or tips that are provided in this book

In the Middle Ages in Europe, daily life was hard, even if you were rich. Read on and learn about what people in those times had to face.

The Middle Ages

The middle ages in Europe started about 500 C.E. with the end of the Roman Empire, and ran until the start of the Renaissance (rebirth) about 1500 C.E. The first centuries were chaotic, as the old systems of empire broke down. It became harder to trade and communicate, and there was no central government to help you out when enemies attacked.

Smaller kingdoms, dukedoms, and independent areas developed, and each had to struggle to figure out how to function.

Over time, almost all of Europe sorted itself into societies that had three broad sections: the nobility, the clergy, and the peasants.

The nobility included the royal family that had the power in the country, the noble families close to the royal family, and other strong, influential, and powerful households. The knights were the specialized fighting troops who worked for the nobility and the local lords.

Family of Carlos IV

The clergy were priests and bishops who served the churches across the land, for most of Europe was Christian. It included many monks and nuns, who lived in their own self-supporting communities, often isolated from the rest of society.

There was no middle class, and no class of wealthy people like we have today. Almost everybody who was not of the nobility or of the clergy was lumped together as peasants. The peasants worked the land and served in the manor houses, castles, and palaces of the nobility.

They built and prepared and repaired everything from mills to barns to weapons of war. When there was a war, many of the men marched off to served as foot soldiers, archers, and other high-risk roles in the army of their local lord.

Life was uncertain and full of threats. Most of the things that we do every day, from making breakfast to dealing with a cut on a finger, took a lot longer and had a more uncertain result.

Life At Home

For the poor, homes were simple and small. The whole family might eat, sleep, and do everything they had to do in a single room in a small building. For those in the towns and cities, the front of the building might be a shop where the family made and sold something like shoes, and they would live in a small room at the back.

There were no flush toilets, no showers, no hair conditioner. You can imagine what the house and the people smelled like.

Monks and nuns lived in separate communities, with very little private space or private property. Priests lived in houses that were better-equipped than those of the peasants they served, but much simpler than those of the nobles. Bishops often had palaces almost as fancy as those of princes.

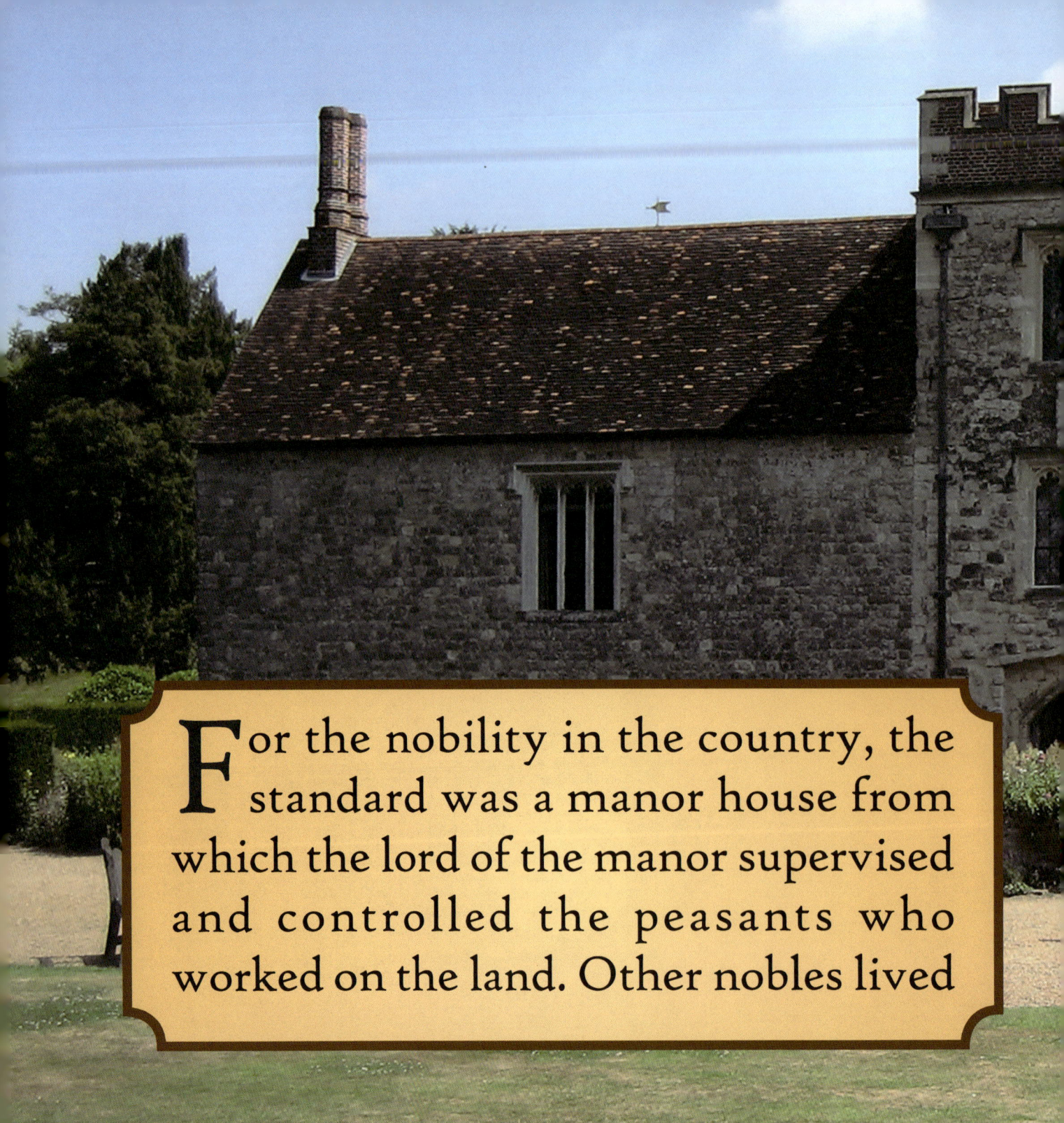

For the nobility in the country, the standard was a manor house from which the lord of the manor supervised and controlled the peasants who worked on the land. Other nobles lived

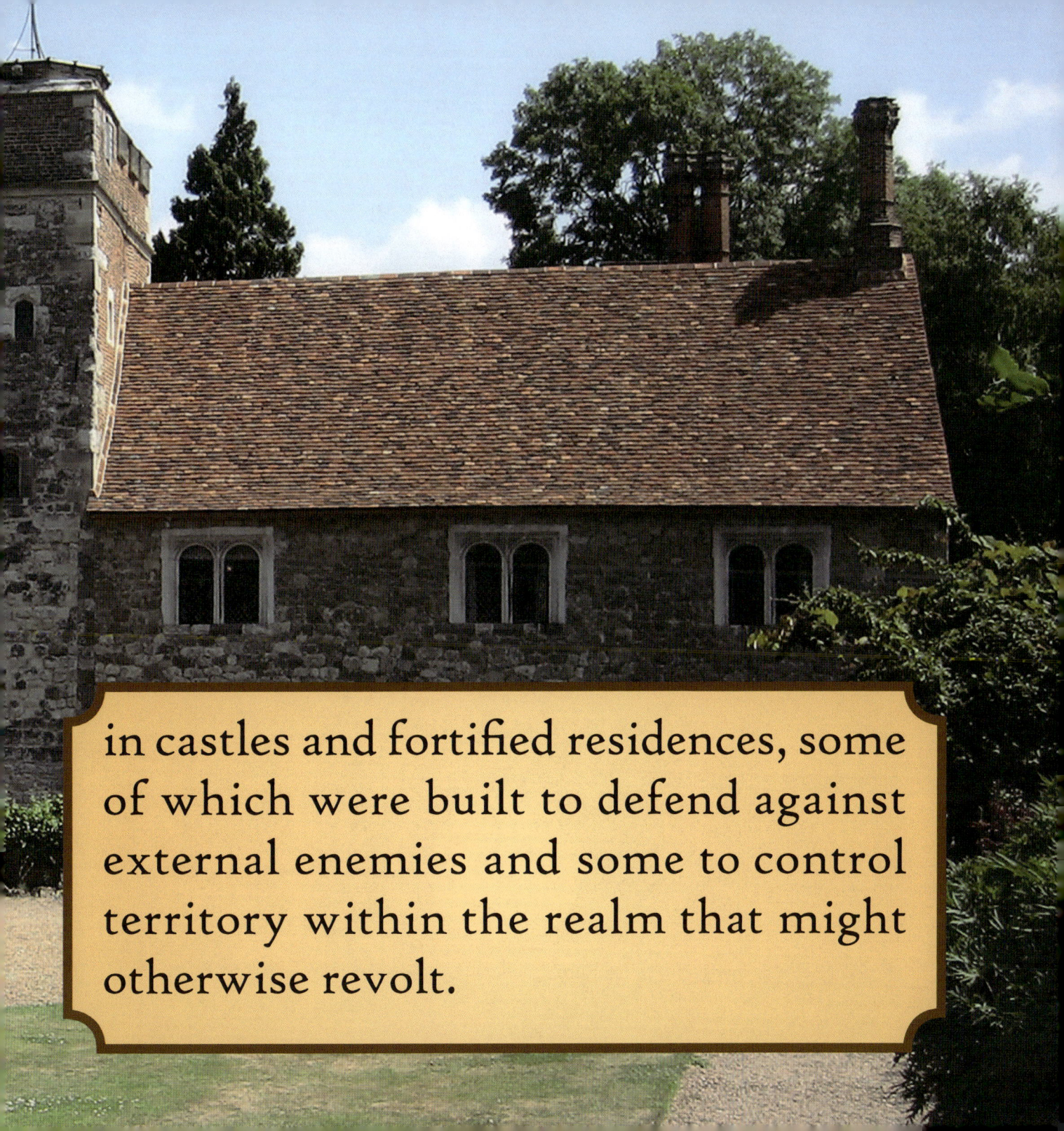

in castles and fortified residences, some of which were built to defend against external enemies and some to control territory within the realm that might otherwise revolt.

But even for the richest lord in the fanciest castle, things were not what we would call comfortable. There was little or no glass, so the windows were either open to the air or covered with skins that dimmed what light came in. Stone buildings were not insulated in any real way, except by tapestries hanging on the inner walls.

The floors were covered with straw or other material and when the straw got too full of garbage, leftover scraps from meals, and waste from animals, the house servants took out and burned the straw and replaced it with a new load. The only heating was by fires in open fireplaces, so the air was smoky and there was a fine layer of soot on every flat surface.

Diet

The good food mostly went to the nobility. They had the best of the meat, the fish, and the fruit as well as rare imported goods. They also had trained chefs who could make the materials into something interesting.

The main meal for the nobility was usually at the end of the day, and was often a feast with many courses of food. This was how the nobles entertained each other, and also part of how they competed to see who could provide the most impressive meal.

Most of the clergy ate a much simpler diet, although the bishops were honorary nobles and often ate as well as princes.

For the peasants, the diet was mainly based on grains, dairy products like eggs and cheese, and vegetables.

They had no way to refrigerate food, so they could only store things that would not rot quickly, like root vegetables and smoked or dried meat and fish.

Work Life

The peasants in the country worked for the local lord. They did everything so the crops would grow and to tend the livestock, with very little beyond hand tools to work with.

The cultivated land bordered wilder woodlands, so on top of the heavy labor, there was the constant possibility that a wolf or other wild animal would try to attack a sheep or a person.

In both the country and the city, the peasants provided household labor. They prepared and cooked food, made clothing, tended fires, created and repaired armor for the knights and soldiers, brought water and took away chamber pots (there were no toilets), turned wool and flax into cloth, and the cloth into clothing, and did whatever else needed to be done.

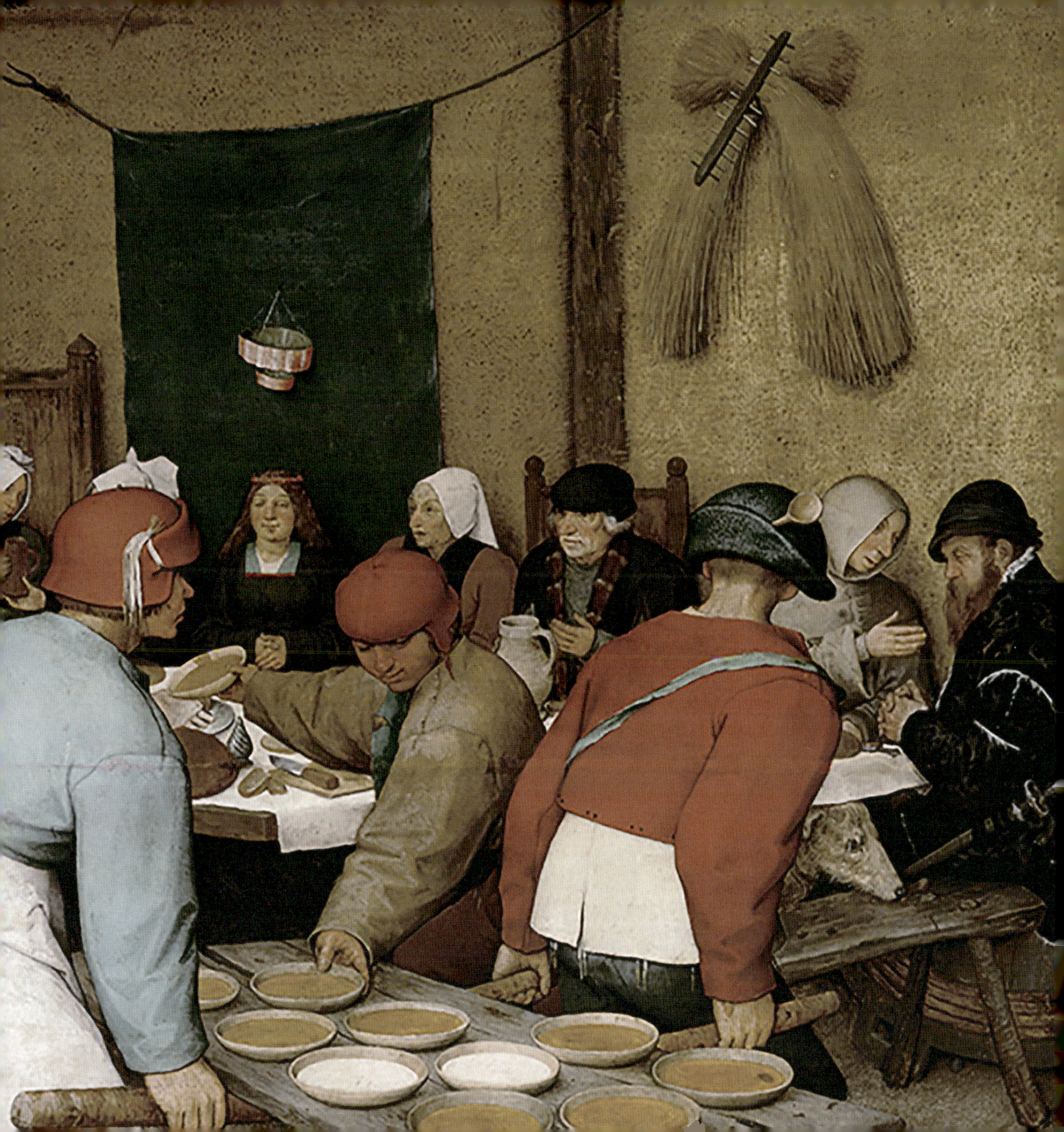

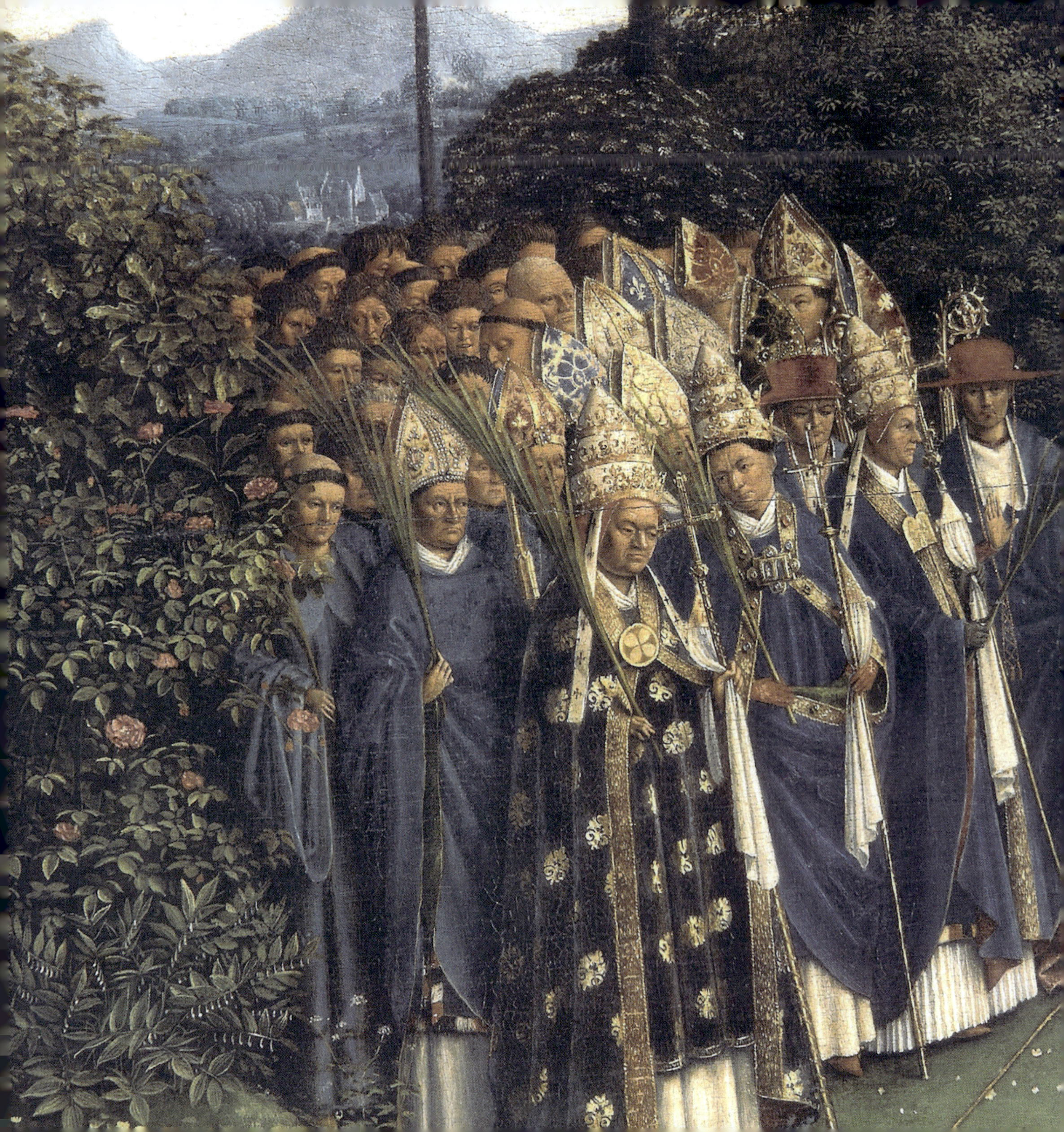

The main job of the clergy was to pray, to lead services, to teach, and to provide sacraments—baptism, marriage, forgiveness, and Christian burial. They also taught and counselled the people in their care, but their overall goal was to help people understand the will of God, so they might live more as God would want them to live.

Festivals and Seasons

Most of Europe was Christian, and all through the year there were festivals and religious observances that broke up the steady flow of work days.

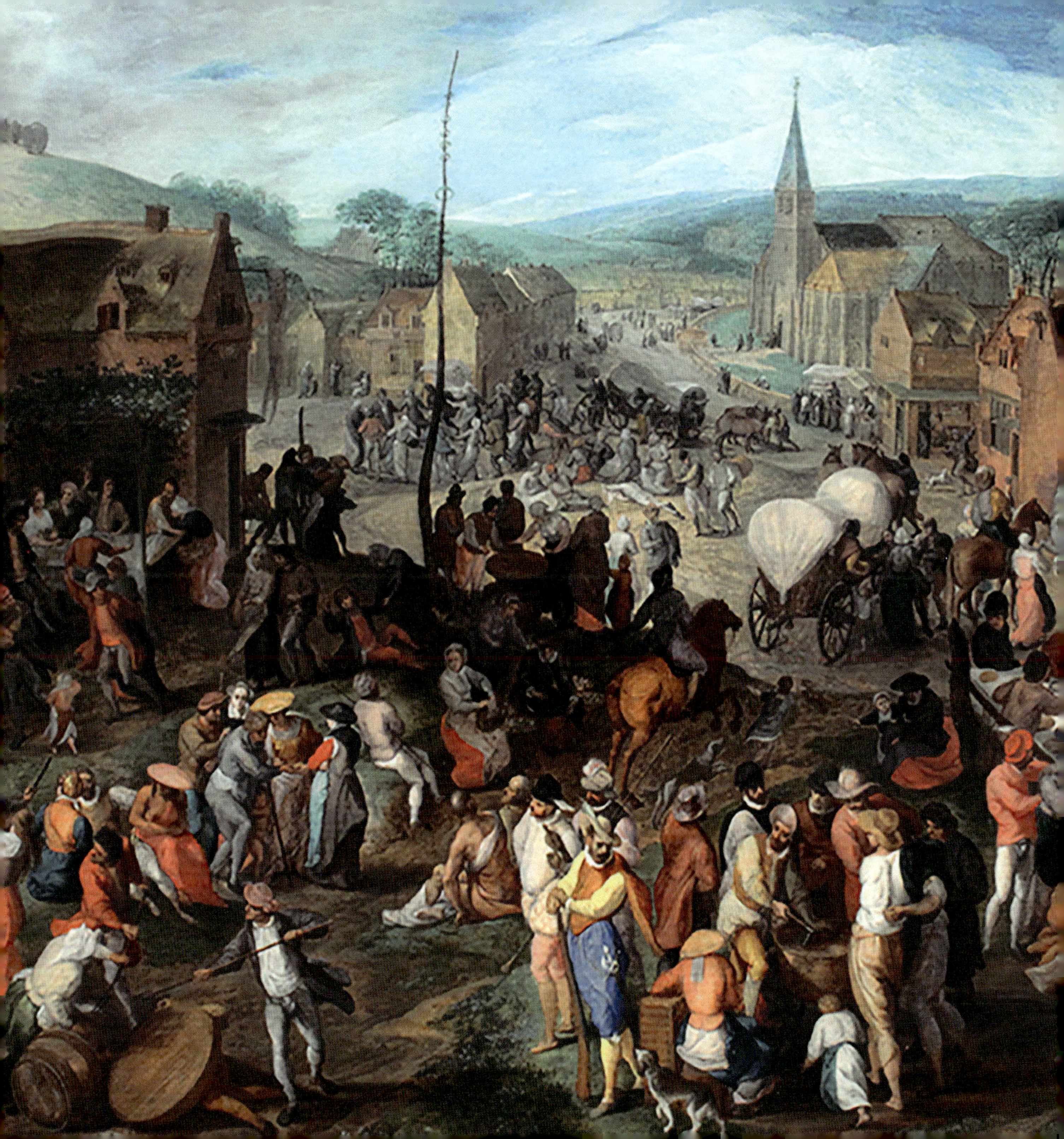

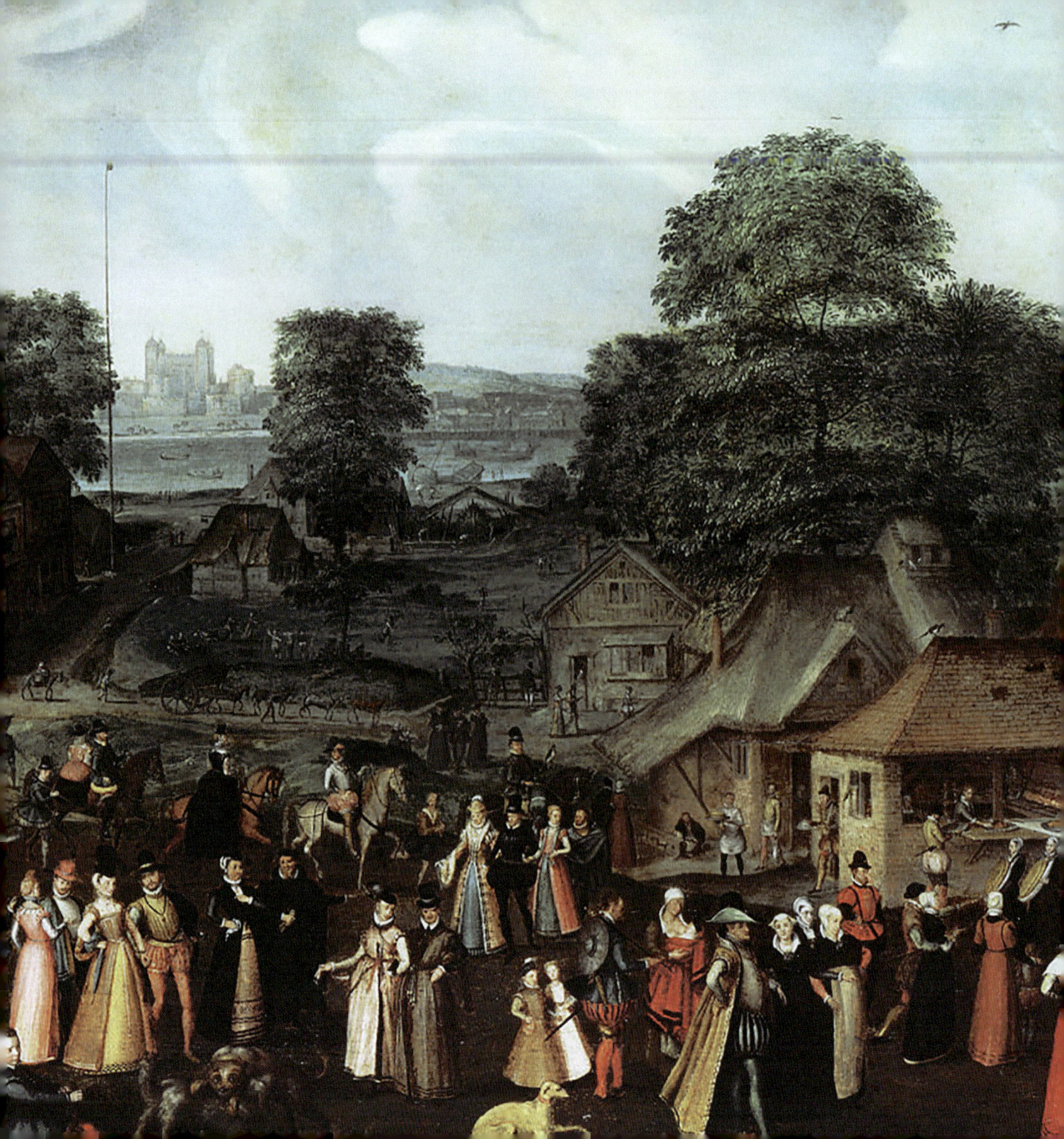

Some historians estimate that, leaving aside Sundays (a day of rest), there were as much as eight weeks' worth of days in every year that were mainly celebrations, festivals, or religious observations.

Education

Education did not exist for the peasants. As soon as a child was old enough, he went to work, both to help support the family and to serve the lord under whom the family lived.

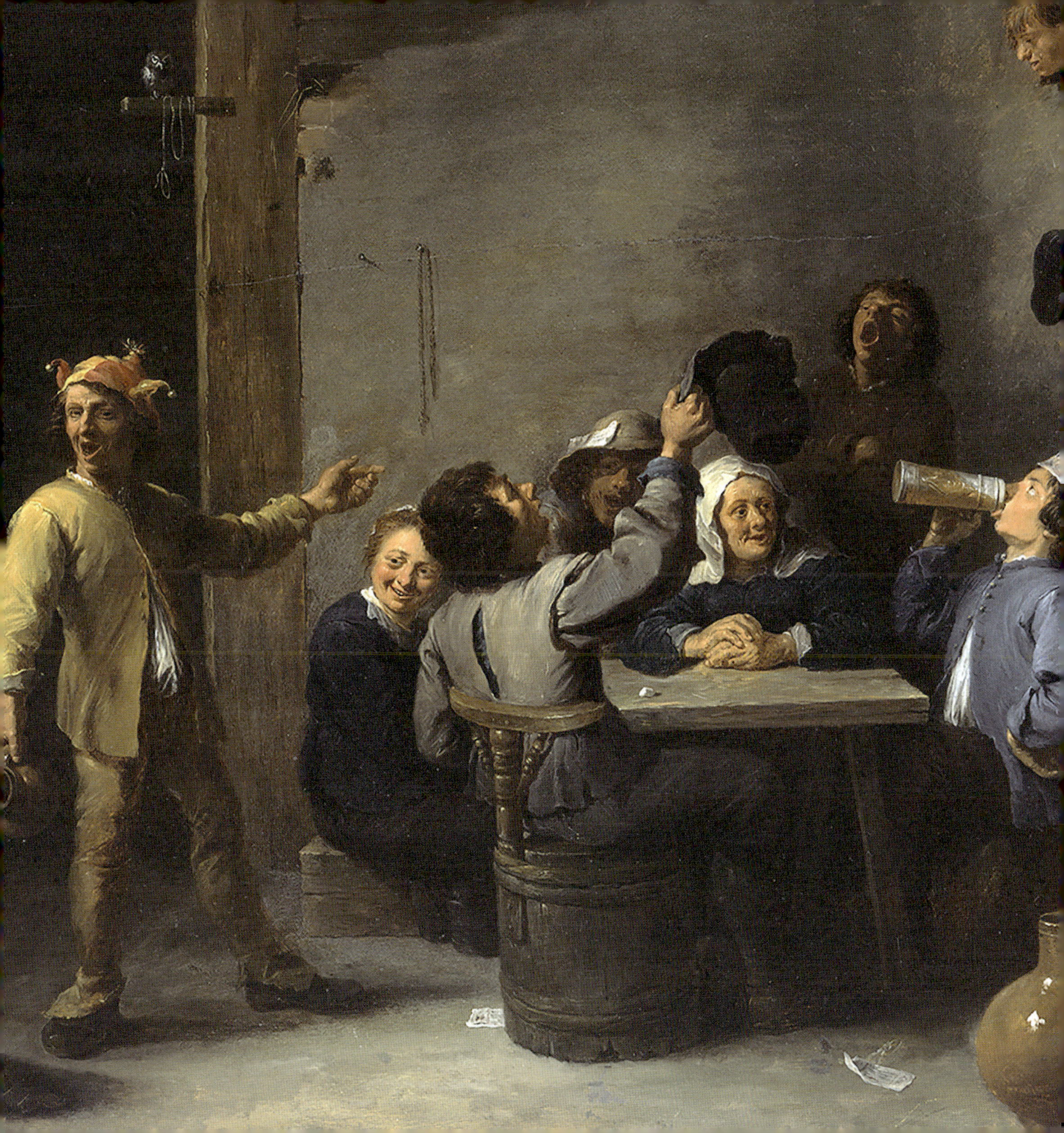

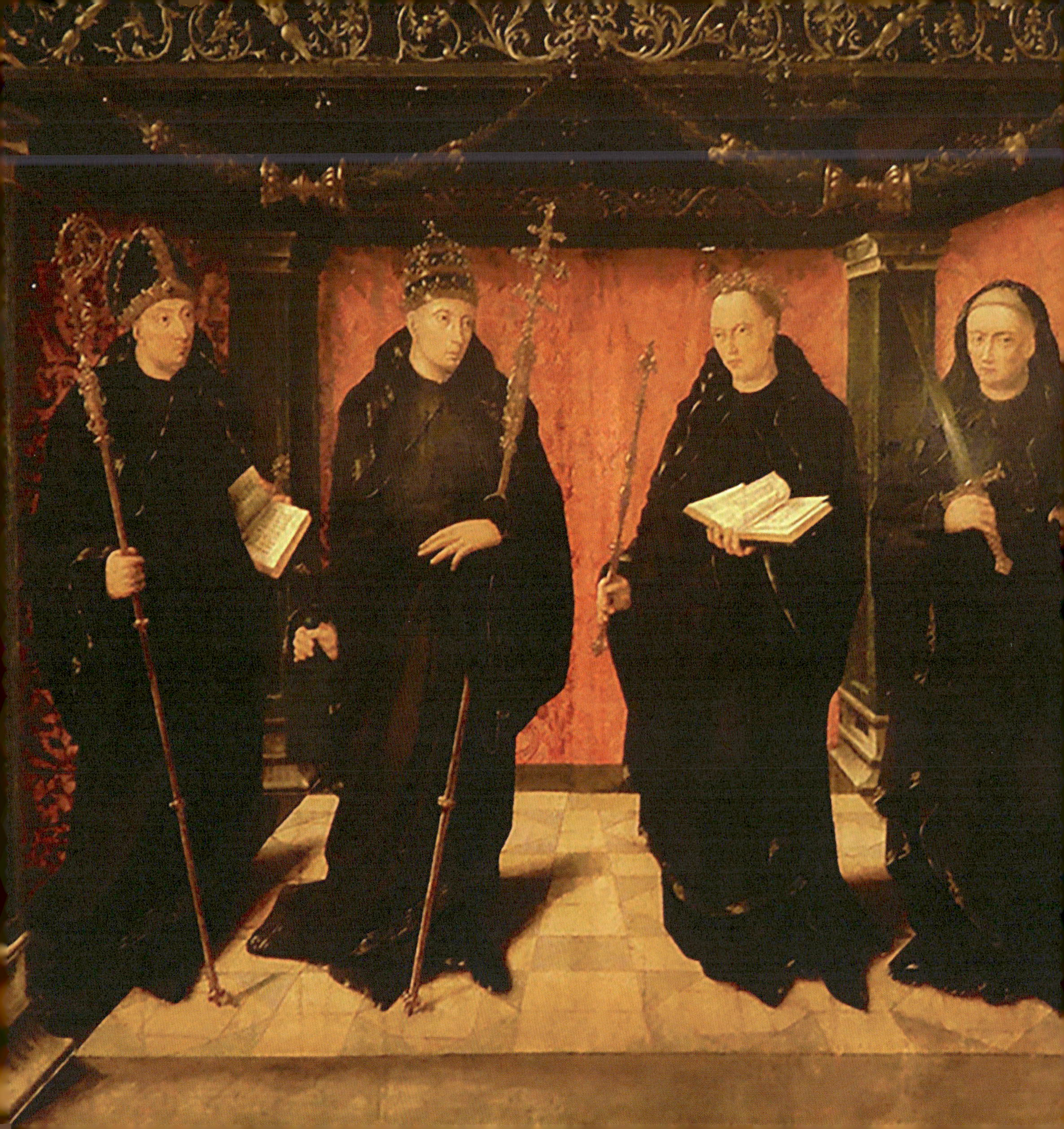

Monks were often scholars and well-educated, and noble families often sent their children to learn from the monks. However, monastic studies concentrated on the Bible and on trying to understand the will of God, and were less concerned with other topics such as medicine, law, or science.

Government

We are used to voting the people who run our government, and having them work under the limits of a constitution that describes their powers and duties. None of that existed in medieval Europe.

The ruler of a country usually got there by inheriting the job from his father, or by conquering the land and taking the crown from the former king.

There were some limits on what a king in power could do. For instance, in England in 1215, the nobles forced King John to agree to the Magna Carta, which described the rights and duties of the nobles in the kingdom, and put some restrictions on what the king could do without agreement from the nobles.

In the same way that the king had great power over the people and the land, each local lord had power over the knights who served him and the peasants in his territory. The lord could seize property, compel people to work for him, and even execute people based on his own decision.

Staying on the right side of your lord was very important!

Health

In medieval times, people had little understanding of what caused good and bad health. People did not know anything about germs or infection; they did not know that if you washed your hands regularly you had a better chance of staying healthy.

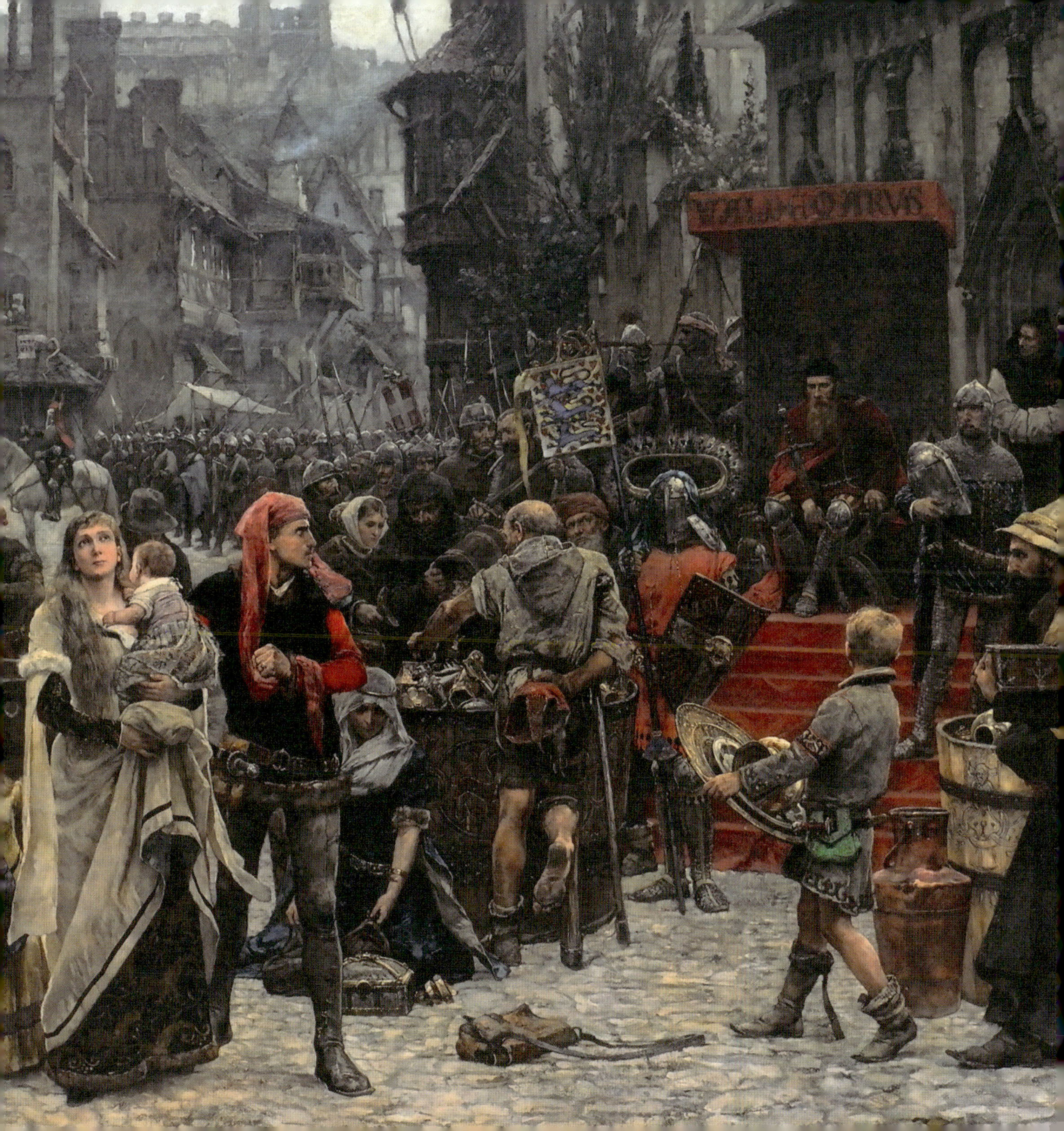

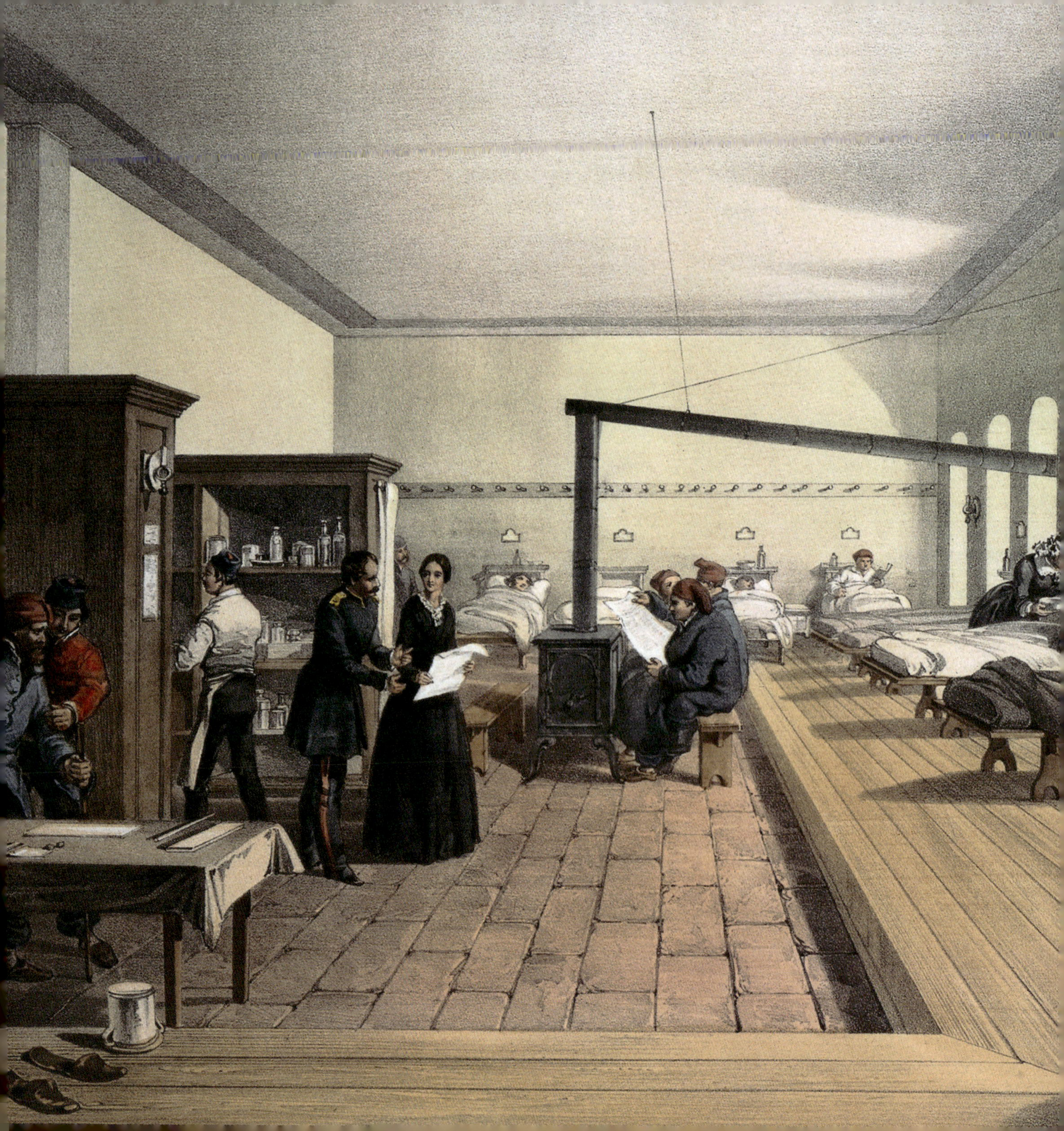

They did not understand about how blood flowed in the body, or how the brain sent signals to the hands and got information from your eyes or nose.

There were traditional medicines that worked well to counter many illnesses, but they were helpless against major illnesses, like the Black Death, that periodically killed off large segments of the population.

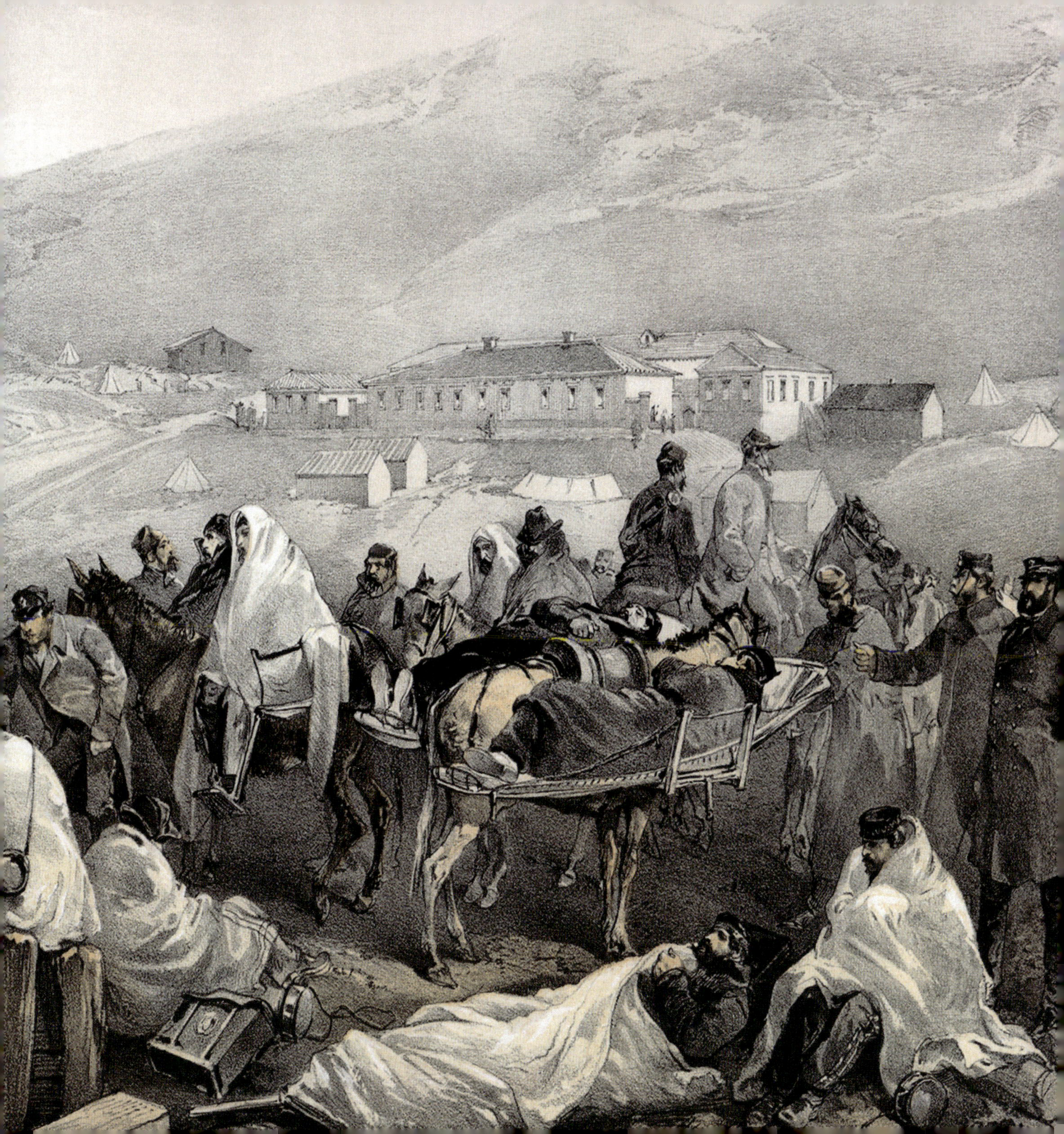

Even the rich and powerful lived in fear of illnesses that they did not know how to avoid.

More About Medieval Life

There is much more to learn about the goods and bads of life in the middle ages in Europe. Read Baby Professor books like *Why Were Castles Built?* and *How to Become a Knight* to learn even more.

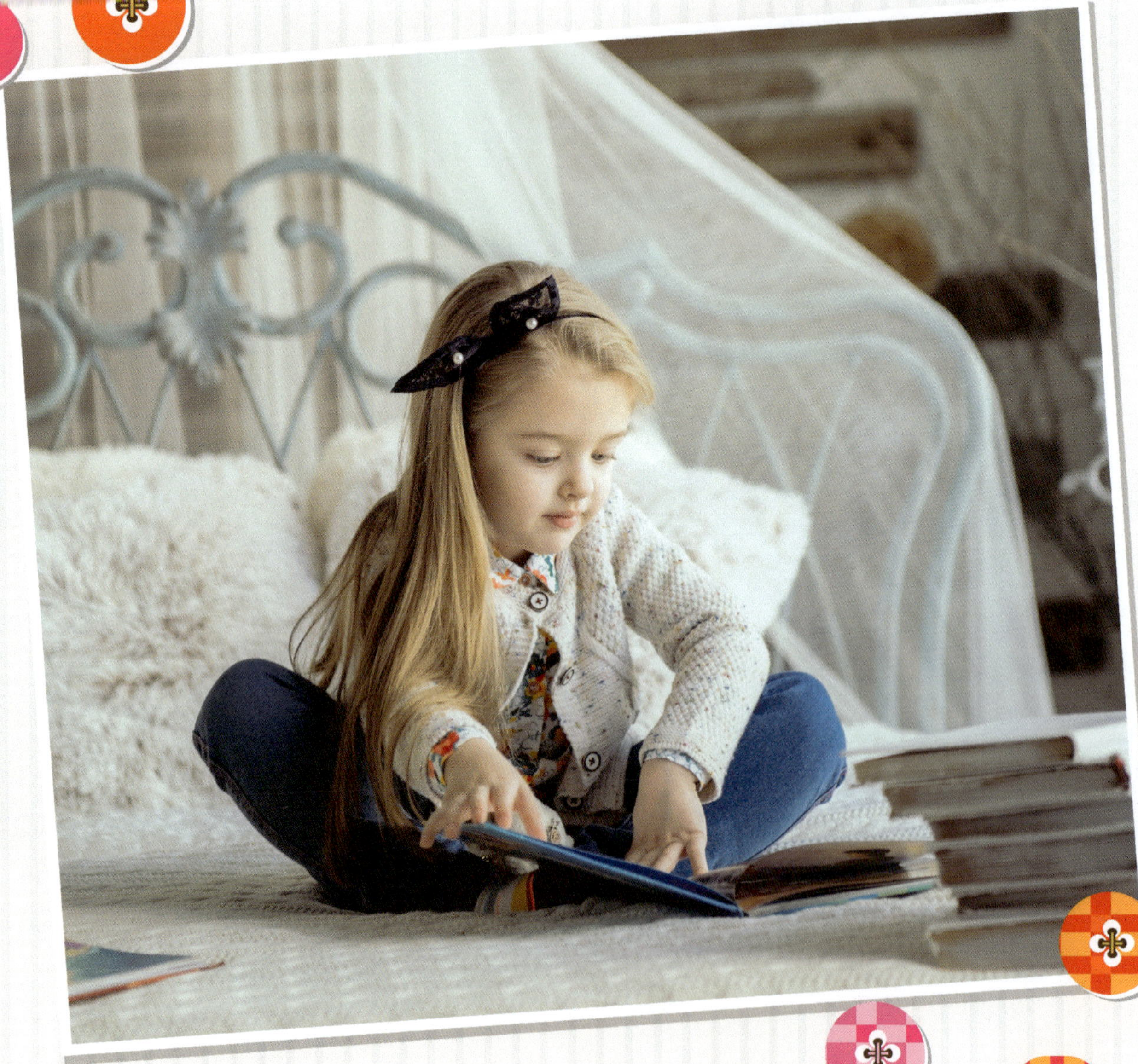

Visit

BABY PROFESSOR
EDUCATION KIDS

www.BabyProfessorBooks.com

to download Free Baby Professor eBooks
and view our catalog of new and exciting
Children's Books

Printed in Great Britain
by Amazon

Published by
Speedy Publishing LLC
40 E. Main St., #1156
Newark DE 19711

Cover by 24HR Covers

ISBN 9781541913134